Some Memoirs of

CW01497224

Some Memoirs of the Life of Job, the Son of Solomon, the High Priest of Boonda in Africa; Who was a Slave About Two Years in Maryland; and Afterwards Being Brought to England, was Set Free, and Sent to His Native Land in the Year 1734

Thomas Bluett

SOME
MEMOIRS
OF THE
LIFE of *JOB*,
THE
SON of *SOLOMON*
THE
HIGH PRIEST of *Boonda*
in *Africa*;

Who was a Slave about two Years
in *Maryland*; and afterwards being
brought to *England*, was set free,
and sent to his native Land in the
Year 1734.

By THOMAS BLUETT, *Gent.*
who was intimately acquainted with him
in *America*, and came over to *England*
with him.

LONDON:
Printed for RICHARD FORD, at the *Angel* in the *Poultry*,
over against the *Compter*. M.DCC.XXXIV.
(Price One Shilling.)

SOME
MEMOIRS
OF THE
LIFE of JOB,
THE
SON of SOLOMON
THE
HIGH PRIEST of Boonda
in Africa;
Who was a Slave about two Years
in Maryland; and afterwards being
brought to England, was set free,
and sent to his native Land in the Year
1734.

By THOMAS BLUETT, Gent.
who was intimately acquainted with him
in America, and came over to England
with him.

LONDON:
Printed for RICHARD FORD, at the Angel in
the Poultry,
over against the Compter. M.DCC.XXXIV.

TO THE
Right Honble. His GRACE the
Duke of Montague.

May it please your GRACE,

JOB, Son of the High Priest of Boonda in Africa, (being gratefully sensible of the repeated Favours he had received from Your GRACE) requested me to write an Account of him, and to lay the fame before You, as an Acknowledgment of your GRACE'S great Humanity and Goodness to an unfortunate Stranger; Virtues which distinguish Your GRACE'S Character, and add the noblest Lustre to the most exalted Dignities and Honours.

Pursuant to my Promise to him, I have drawn up the following ACCOUNT; which I humbly beg Leave to present to Your GRACE'S Protection.

I am very sensible the Imperfections of it are many; but hope Your GRACE will pardon them, especially as I have not been us'd to such Matters as these. The Facts I I have inserted, are what I had by JOB's particular Information, or from my own Knowledge; and if it meets

with Your GRACE'S Approbation, it will fully
answer the Design of,

May it please your GRACE,
Your GRACE'S most Obedient,
and most Humble Servant,

Thomas Bluett.

THE
CONTENTS.

SOME
MEMOIRS
OF THE
LIFE of JOB, &c.

INTRODUCTION.

HAVING had occasion to inform my self of many considerable and curious Circumstances of the Life of JOB, the African Priest, in a more exact and particular Manner than the Generality of his Acquaintance in England could do; I was desired by himself, a little before his Departure, to draw up an Account of him agreeable to the Information he had given me at different Times, and to the Truth of the Facts, which I had either been a Witness to, or personally concerned in upon his Account. I have been solicited also by several Gentlemen, who were Benefactors to JOB, to publish what I knew of him: And I am of opinion such an Account is pretty generally wanted; at least it cannot but be agreeable to those Persons, who were pleased to do kind Offices to this Stranger, merely from a Principle of Humanity, before any particular Account of him could be had. Therefore I have at length resolved to communicate to the

World such Particulars of the Life and Character of this African Gentleman, as I think will be most useful and entertaining; intending to advance nothing as Fact, but what I either knew to be such, or have had from JOB's own Mouth, whose Veracity I have no reason to doubt of.

SECT. I.

An Account of the Family of JOB; his Education; and the more remarkable Circumstances of his Life, before he was taken Captive.

JOB's Countrymen, like the Eastern People and some others, use to design themselves by the Names of their Ancestors, and in their Appellations mention their Progenitors several Degrees backward; tho' they also have Sirnames for distinguishing their particular Families, much after the same Manner as in England. JOB's Name, in his own Country, is HYUBA, BOON SALUMENA, BOON HIBRAHEMA; i.e. JOB, the Son of Solomon, the Son of Abraham. The Sirname of his Family is Jallo.

JOB, who is now about 31 or 32 Years of age, was born at a Town called Boonda in the County of Galumbo (in our Maps Catumbo) in the Kingdom of Futa in Africa; which lies on both Sides the River Senegal, and on the south Side reaches as far as, the River Gambia. These two Rivers, JOB assured me, run pretty near parallel to one another, and never meet, contrary to the Position they have in most of our Maps. The Eastern Boundary of the

Kingdom of Futa or Senega is the great Lake, called in our Maps Lacus Guarde. The Extent of it, towards the North, is not so certain. The chief City or Town of it is Tombut; over against which, on the other side of the River, is Boonda, the Place of JOB's Nativity.

About fifty Years ago Hibrahim, the Grandfather of JOB, founded the Town of Boonda, in the Reign of Bubaker, then King of Futa, and was, by his Permission, sole Lord Proprietor and Governor of it, and at the same Time High Priest, or Alpha; so that he had a Power to make what Laws and Regulations he thought proper for the Increase and good Government of his new City. Among other Institutions, one was, that no Person who flies thither for Protection shall be made a Slave. This Privilege is in force there to this Day, and is extended to all in general, that can read and know God, as they express it; and it has contributed much to the Peopling of the Place, which is now very large and flourishing. Some time after the Settlement of this Town Hibrahim died; and, as the Priesthood is hereditary there, Salumen his Son, the Father of JOB, became High Priest. About the same Time Bubaker the King dying, his Brother Gelazi, who was next Heir, succeeded him.

Gelazi had a Son, named Sambo, whom he put under the Care of Salumen, JOB's Father, to learn the Koran and Arabick Language. JOB was at this Time also with his Father, was Companion to Sambo, and studied along with him. Sambo, upon the Death of Gelazi, was made King of Futa, and reigns there at present. When JOB was fifteen Years old, he assisted his Father as Emaum, or Sub-priest. About this Age he married the Daughter of the Alpha of Tombut, who was then only eleven Years old. By her he had a Son (when she was thirteen Years old) called Abdolah; and after that two more Sons, called Hibrahim and Sambo. About two Years before his Captivity he married a second Wife, Daughter of the Alpha of Tomga; by whom he has a Daughter named Fatima, after the Daughter of their Prophet Mahommed. Both these Wives, with their Children, were alive when he came from Home.

SECT. II.

Of the Manner of his being taken Captive; and what
followed upon it, till his Return.

IN February, 1730. JOB's Father hearing of
an English Ship at Gambia River, sent him,
with two Servants to attend him, to sell two
Negroes and to buy Paper, and some other
Necessaries; but desired him not to venture
over the River, because the Country of the
Mandingoes, who are Enemies to the People of
Futa, lies on the other side. JOB not agreeing
with Captain Pike (who commanded the Ship,
lying then at Gambia, in the Service of Captain
Henry Hunt, Brother to Mr. William Hunt,
Merchant, in Little Tower-Street, London) sent
back the two Servants to acquaint his Father
with it, and to let him know that he intended to
go farther. Accordingly, having agreed with
another Man, named Loumein Yoas, who
understood the Mandingoe Language, to go
with him as his Interpreter, he crossed the
River Gambia, and disposed of his Negroes for
some Cows. As he was returning Home, he
stopp'd for some Refreshment at the House of
an old Acquaintance; and the Weather being
hot, he hung up his Arms in the House, while
he refresh'd himself. Those Arms were very

valuable; consisting of a Gold-hilted Sword, a Gold Knife, which they wear by their Side, and a rich Quiver of Arrows, which King Sambo had made him a Present of. It happened that a Company of the Mandingoes, who live upon Plunder, passing by at that Time, and observing him unarmed, rush'd in, to the Number of seven or eight at once, at a back Door, and pinioned JOB, before he could get to his Arms, together with his Interpreter, who is a Slave in Maryland still. They then shaved their Heads and Beards, which JOB and his Man resented as the highest Indignity; tho' the Mandingoes meant no more by it, than to make them appear like Slaves taken in War. On the 27th of February, 1730. they carried them to Captain Pike at Gambia, who purchased them; and on the first of March they were put on Board. Soon after JOB found means to acquaint Captain Pike that he was the same Person that came to trade with him a few Days before, and after what Manner he had been taken. Upon this Captain Pike gave him leave to redeem himself and his Man; and JOB sent to an Acquaintance of his Father's, near Gambia, who promised to send to JOB's Father, to inform him of what had happened, that he might take some Course to have him set at

Liberty. But it being a Fortnight's journey between that Friend's House and his Father's, and the Ship failing in about a Week after, JOB was brought with the rest of the Slaves to Annapolis in Maryland, and delivered to Mr. Vachell Denton, Factor to Mr. Hunt, before mentioned. JOB heard since, by Vessels that came from Gambia, that his Father sent down several Slaves, a little after Captain Pike failed, in order to procure his Redemption; and that Sambo, King of Futa, had made War upon the Mandingoes, and cut off great Numbers of them, upon account of the Injury they had done to his Schoolfellow.

Mr. Vachell Denton sold JOB to one Mr. Tolsey in Kent Island in Maryland, who put him to work in making Tobacco; but he was soon convinced that JOB had never been used to such Labour. He every Day shewed more and more Uneasiness under this Exercise, and at last grew sick, being no way able to bear it; so that his Master was obliged to find easier Work for him, and therefore put him to tend the Cattle. JOB would often leave the Cattle, and withdraw into the Woods to pray; but a white Boy frequently watched him, and whilst he was at his Devotion would mock him, and throw Dirt in his Face. This very much disturbed JOB, and added to his other Misfortunes; all which were increased by his Ignorance of the English Language, which prevented his complaining, or telling his Case to any Person about him. Grown in some measure desperate, by reason of his present Hardships, he resolved to travel at a Venture; thinking he might possibly be taken up by some Master, who would use him better, or otherwise meet with some lucky Accident, to divert or abate his Grief. Accordingly, he travelled thro' the Woods, till he came to the County of Kent, upon Delaware Bay, now esteemed Part of Pensilvania; altho' it is properly a Part of Maryland, and belongs to my Lord Baltimore. There is a Law in force, throughout the Colonies of Virginia, Maryland, Pensilvania, &c. as far as Boston in New England, viz. That any Negroe, or white Servant who is not known in the County, or has no Pass, may be secured by any Person, and kept in the common Goal, till the Master of such Servant shall fetch him. Therefore JOB being able to give no Account of himself, was put in Prison there.

This happened about the Beginning of June, 1731. when I, who was attending the Courts there, and had heard of JOB, went with several Gentlemen to the Goaler's House, being a Tavern, and desired to see him. He was brought into the Tavern to us, but could not speak one Word of English. Upon our Talking and making Signs to him, he wrote a Line or two before us, and when he read it, pronounced the Words Allah and Mahommed; by which, and his refusing a Glass of Wine we offered him, we perceived he was a Mahometan, but could not imagine of what Country he was, or how he got thither; for by his affable Carriage, and the easy Composure of his Countenance, we could perceive he was no common Slave.

When JOB had been some time confined, an old Negroe Man, who lived in that Neighbourhood, and could speak the Jalloff Language, which JOB also understood, went to him, and conversed with him. By this Negroe the Keeper was informed to whom JOB belonged, and what was the Cause of his leaving his Master. The Keeper thereupon wrote to his Master, who soon after fetch'd him home, and was much kinder to him than before; allowing him a Place to pray in, and some other Conveniencies, in order to make his Slavery as easy as possible. Yet Slavery and Confinement was by no means agreeable to

JOB, who had never been used to it; he therefore wrote a Letter in Arabick to his Father,

acquainting him with his Misfortunes, hoping he might yet find Means to redeem him. This Letter he sent to Mr. Vachell Denton, desiring it might be sent to Africa by Captain Pike; but he being gone to England, Mr. Denton sent the Letter inclosed to Mr. Hunt, in order to be sent to Africa by Captain Pike from England; but Captain Pike had sailed for Africa before the Letter came to Mr. Hunt, who therefore kept it in his own Hands, till he should have a proper Opportunity of sending it. It happened that this Letter was seen by James Oglethorpe, Esq; who, according to his usual Goodness and Generosity, took Compassion on JOB, and gave his Bond to Mr. Hunt for the Payment of a certain Sum, upon the Delivery of JOB here in England. Mr. Hunt upon this sent to Mr. Denton, who purchas'd him again of his Master for the same Money which Mr. Denton had formerly received for him; his Master being very willing to part with him, as finding him no ways fit for his Business.

He lived some time with Mr. Denton at Annapolis, before any Ship could stir out, upon account of the Ice that lay in all the Rivers of Maryland at that Time. In this Interval he became acquainted with the Reverend Mr. Henderson, a Gentleman of great Learning, Minister of Annapolis, and Commissary to the Bishop of London, who gave JOB the Character of a Person of great Piety and Learning; and indeed his good Nature and Affability gain'd him many Friends besides in that Place.

In March, 1733. he set sail in the William, Captain George Uriel Commander; in which Ship I was also a Passenger. The Character which the Captain and I had of him at Annapolis, induced us to teach him as much of the English Language as we could, he being then able to speak but few Words of it, and those hardly intelligible. This we set about as soon as we were out at Sea, and in about a Fortnight's Time taught him all his Letters, and to spell almost any single Syllable, when distinctly pronounced to him; but JOB and my self falling sick, we were hindered from making any greater Progress at that Time. However, by the Time that we arrived in England, which was the latter End of April, 1733. he had learned so much of our Language, that he was able to understand most of what we said in common Conversation; and we that were used to his Manner of Speaking, could make shift to understand him tolerably well. During the Voyage, he was very constant in his Devotions; which he never omitted, on any Pretence, notwithstanding we had exceeding bad Weather all the time we were at Sea. We often permitted him to kill our fresh Stock, that he might eat of it himself; for he eats no Flesh, unless he has killed the Animal with his own Hands, or knows that it has been killed by some Mussulman. He has no Scruple about Fish; but won't touch a bit of Pork, it being expresly forbidden by their Law. By his good Nature and Affability he gained the good Will of all the Sailors, who (not to mention other kind Offices) all the way up the Channel shewed him the Head Lands and remarkable Places; the Names of which JOB wrote down carefully, together with the Accounts that were given him about them. His Reason for so doing, he told me, was, that if he met with any Englishman in his Country, he might by these Marks be able to convince him that he had been in England.

On our Arrival in England, we heard that Mr. Oglethorpe was gone to Georgia, and that Mr. Hunt had provided a Lodging for JOB at

Limehouse. After I had visited my Friends in the Country, I went up on purpose to see JOB. He was, very sorrowful, and told me, that Mr. Hunt had been applied to by some Persons to sell him, who pretended they would send him home; but he feared they would either sell him again as a Slave, or if they sent him home would expect an unreasonable Ransom for him. I took him to London with me, and waited on Mr. Hunt, to desire leave to carry him to Cheshunt in Hartfordshire; which Mr. Hunt comply'd with. He told me he had been apply'd to, as JOB had suggested, but did not intend to part with him without his own Consent; but as Mr. Oglethorpe was out of England, if any of JOB's Friends would pay the Money, he would accept of it, provided they would undertake to send him home safely to his own Country. I also obtained his Promise that he would not dispose of him till he heard farther from me.

JOB, while he was at Cheshunt, had the Honour to be sent for by most of the Gentry of that Place, who were mightily pleased with his Company, and concerned for his Misfortunes. They made him several handsome Presents, and proposed that a Subscription should be made for the Payment of the Money to Mr.

Hunt. The Night before we set out for London
from Cheshunt, a Footman belonging to
Samuel Holden, Esq; brought a Letter to JOB,
which was, I think, directed to Sir Byby Lake.
The Letter was delivered at the African House;
upon which the House was pleased to order
that Mr. Hunt should bring in a Bill of the
whole Charges which he had been at about
JOB, and be there paid; which was accordingly
done, and the Sum amounted to Fifty-nine
Pounds, Six Shillings, and eleven Pence Half-
penny. This Sum being paid, Mr. Oglethorpe's
Bond was deliver'd up to the Company. JOB's
Fears were now over, with respect to his being
sold again as a Slave; yet he could not be
persuaded but that he must pay an extravagant
Ramson, when he got home. I confess, I
doubted much of the Success of a Subscription,
the Sum being great, and JOB's Acquaintance
in England being so small; therefore, to ease
JOB's Mind, I spoke to a Gentleman about the
Affair, who has all along been JOB's Friend in a
very remarkable Manner. This Gentleman was
so far from discouraging the Thing, that he
began the Subscription himself with a
handsome Sum, and promised his further
Assistance at a dead Lift. Not to be tedious:
Several Friends, both in London and in the

Country, gave in their charitable Contributions very readily; yet the Sum was so large, that the Subscription was about twenty Pounds short of it; but that generous and worthy Gentleman before mentioned, was pleased to make up the Defect, and the whole Sum was compleated.

I went (being desired) to propose the Matter to the African Company; who, after having heard what I had to say, shew'd me the Orders that the House had made; which were, that JOB should be accommodated at the African House at the Company's Expence, till one of the Company's Ships should go to Gambia, in which he should be sent back to his Friends without any Ransom. The Company then ask'd me, if they could do any Thing more to make JOB easy; and upon my Desire, they order'd, that Mr. Oglethorpe's Bond should be cancelled, which was presently done, and that JOB should have his Freedom in Form, which he received handsomely engross'd with the Company's Seal affixed; after which the full Sum of the whole Charges (viz. Fifty-nine Pounds, Six Shillings, and eleven Pence Half-penny) was paid in to their Clerk, as was before proposed.

JOB's Mind being now perfectly easy, and being himself more known, he went chearfully among his Friends to several Places, both in Town and Country, One Day being at Sir Hans Sloan's, he expressed his great Desire to see the Royal Family. Sir Hans promised to get him introduced, when he had Clothes proper to go in. JOB knew how kind a Friend he had to apply to upon occasion; and he was soon cloathed in a rich silk Dress, made up after his own Country Fashion, and introduced to their Majesties, and the rest of the Royal Family. Her Majesty was pleased to present him with a rich Gold Watch; and the same Day he had the Honour to dine with his Grace the Duke of Mountague, and some others of the Nobility, who were pleased to make him a handsome Present after Dinner. His Grace, after that, was pleased to take JOB often into the Country with him, and shew him the Tools that are necessary for Tilling the Ground, both in Gardens and Fields, and made his Servants shew him how to use them; and afterwards his Grace furnished JOB with all Sorts of such Instruments, and several other rich Presents, which he ordered to be carefully done up in Chests, and put on Board for his Use. 'Tis not possible for me to recollect the many Favours he received from his Grace, and several other Noblemen and Gentlemen, who shewed a singular Generosity towards him; only, I may say in general, that the Goods which were given him, and which he carried over with him, were worth upwards of 500 Pounds; besides which, he was well furnished with Money, in case any Accident should oblige him to go on Shore, or occasion particular Charges at Sea. About the latter End of July last he embark'd on Board one of the African Company's Ships, bound for Gambia; where we hope he is safely arrived, to the great Joy of his Friends, and the Honour of the English Nation.

SECT. III.

Some Observations, as related by JOB, concerning the Manners and Opinions of his Countrymen.

I Don't pretend here, as I hinted before, to trouble the Reader or my self with a full and regular History of JOB's Country. Those who have the Curiosity to inform themselves more particularly in the History of those Parts of the World, may consult the Voyages that are already published on that Subject. I shall only take Notice of some occasional Remarks upon the Customs of the Country, as I had them in Conversation from JOB himself.

It is pretty commonly known that the Africans in general, especially those in the inland Countries, are inured from their Infancy to a hard and low Life, being great Strangers to the Luxury and Delicacy of most of the Countries of Europe. They have the Necessaries of Life, 'tis true, and might have many of the Conveniences of it too; but such is the Simplicity of their Manners, occasioned chiefly by their Ignorance, and want of Correspondence with the politer Part of the World, that they seem contented enough with their plain Necessaries, and don't much hanker after greater Matters, tho' their Country in many Places is capable of great Improvements.

In JOB's Country the Slaves, and poorer sort of People, are employed in preparing the Bread, Corn, &c. And here they labour under a great many Difficulties, having no proper Instruments either for Tilling the Ground, or reaping the Corn when it is ripe; insomuch that they us'd, in Harvest-time, to pull it up, Roots and all. To reduce their Corn to Flower, they rub it between two Stones with their Hands, which must be very tedious. Nor is their Fatigue in Building and Carriage less, for they perform the whole by mere Dint of Strength, and downright Labour. The better Sort of People, who apply themselves to Study and Reading, are obliged to read whole Nights together by the Light of the Fire, (having no Candles or Lamps, as we have) which must be very troublesome in that hot, sultry Country. These, and several other Difficulties which these People labour under, we hope will be removed by JOB's Return; his Friends here having suited their Presents very judiciously to the Necessities of his Country-men; and there is scarce any Tool or Machine, that can be of real Use to them, which JOB has not had from some Friend or other, and their several Uses have been shewn to him with a great deal of Care.

Some of those People spend a great Part of their Time in Hunting; particularly after the Elephants, with whose Teeth they drive a great Trade. One of those Hunters affirmed to JOB, that he had seen an Elephant surprize a Lion (to which Beast, it seems, the Elephant bears a very great Hatred) and carry him to a Tree, which he split down, and putting the Lion's Head thro', let the Tree close again on the Lion's Neck, and there left him to perish. JOB did not say that he knew this Fact to be true; but it seems to be the more probable, upon account of what he assured me he had been a Witness to himself, viz. that an Elephant having catch'd a Lion, carried him directly to a great Slough, and thrusting the Lion's Head under the Mud, held him there till he was smothered.

One Day JOB finding a Cow of his Father's, that had been killed, and partly devoured, resolved, if possible, to surprize the Devourer. Accordingly he placed himself in a Tree, near the Remains of the Cow; and, in the Close of the Evening, he saw two Lions making up to it with great Caution, moving slow, and looking carefully about them. At last one came up, which JOB shot with a poisoned Arrow, and wounded so deadly that he fell immediately upon the Spot; the other coming up soon after, JOB shot another Arrow, and wounded him; upon which he roared out and fled, but the next Morning was found dead about 300 Yards from the Place.

The Poison they dip their Arrows in, is the juice of a certain Tree; and is of such a Nature, that it infects the Blood in a short Time, and makes the Creature quite stupid and senseless. Altho' it is so deadly a Poison, it does not hinder their eating the Flesh of the Animal that is shot; for as soon as it is stupified enough to drop down, they catch it, cut its Throat, &c. as their Law directs, and then eat it. If a Man is wounded with one of these Arrows, they have an Herb, which, if immediately apply'd is a sure Remedy, and extracts the Poison.

And here I would observe two Things, as well from my own Observations abroad, as from what I have just mentioned. First, that in all Countries, where these wild Beasts are, at least where I have been, Providence has so ordered it, that they will all fly at the Sight of a Man, and will never attack him, if they have any room to escape by Flight. Secondly, that all Poisons, of what Nature soever, have their Antidotes generally near them. One Instance of which I shall mention, as being somewhat extraordinary.

The Milk, or Liquor that is squeezed from the Caffavi, or Caffader Roots (of which Roots is made the Bread of that Name, used in Barbadoes, Jamaica, all the Leward, Caribbe Islands) is so deadly a Poison, that one Pint of it will soon kill any Creature that drinks it. Yet I knew a Cow, which drank a hearty Draught of it, and immediately (as if sensible of the Danger she was in) went and fed on a Shrub, which grows common there, called the sensible Plant, from the shrivelling up of its Leaves upon the least Touch; and altho' we expected every Minute to see her fall down dead, it so expelled the Poison, that the received not she least Hurt by it.

The Manner of their Marriages and Baptisms is something remarkable. When a Man has a mind to marry his Son (which they generally do much sooner than in England) and has found out a suitable Match for him, he goes to the Girl's Father, proposes the Matter to him, and agrees for the Price that he is to pay for her; which the Father of the Woman always gives to her as a Dowry. All Things being concluded on, the two Fathers and the young Man go to the Priest, and declare their Agreement; which finishes the Marriage. But now comes the great Difficulty, viz. how the Young Man shall get his Wife home; for the Women, Cousins, and Relations, take on mightily, and guard the Door of the House, to prevent her being carried away; but at last the young Man's Presents and Generosity to them, makes them abate their Grief. He then provides a Friend, well mounted, to carry her off; but as soon as she is up on Horseback, the Women renew their Lamentations, and rush in to dismount her. However, the Man is generally successful, and rides off with his Prize to the House provided for her. After this they make a Treat for their Friends, but the Woman never appears at it; and tho' the Ladies here in England are generally more free after Marriage than before, with the Women in JOB's Country it is quite contrary; for they are so very bashful, that they will never permit their Husbands to see them without a Vail on for three Years after they are married; insomuch, that altho' JOB has a Daughter by his last Wife, yet he never saw her unveiled since Marriage, having been married to her but about two Years before he came from home. To prevent Quarrels, and keep Peace among their Wives, the Husbands divide their Time equally betwixt them; and are so exact in this Affair, that if one Wife lies in, the Husband lies alone in her Apartment those Nights, that are her Turn, and not with the other Wife. If a Wife proves very bad, they put her away, and she keeps her Dowry, and any one may marry her after her Divorce; but they don't use to put them away upon slight Occasions. If a Woman puts away her Husband, she must return him her Dowry; and she is look'd upon always after as a scandalous Person, no Man caring to have any thing to do with her.

All their Male Children are circumcised; but, besides, they have a kind of Baptism for all Children, of both Sexes. When the Child is seven Days old, the People that are invited meet together at the Father's House; the Father names the Child, and the Priest writes the Name of the Child on a piece of smooth Board. Then the Father kills a Cow or Sheep, according to his Ability; part of which is dress'd for the Company, and the rest distributed amongst the Poor: After which the Child is wash'd all over with fair Water, and

then the Priest writes the Child's Name on
Paper, which is rolled up, and tied about the
Child's Neck; where it remains, till it is wore or
rubb'd off.

The Ceremony at their Burials has nothing
remarkable in it. They put the dead Body in the
Earth, and cover it up as we do in England,
saying some Prayers over it, which JOB told
me were intended only for the Benefit of the
Bystanders, and not of the dead Person; for
they are not of opinion that the Dead can reap
any Advantage by their Devotion at that Time.

Their Opinions and Traditions, in Matters
of Religion, are much the same with those of
the Generality of the Mahometans; tho' the
learned Sort of them give a more plausible and
refined Turn to the gross and sensual Doctrines
of the Koran, than those in Turkey, and some
other Places. They have a strong Aversion to
the least Appearance of Idolatry, insomuch
that they will not keep a Picture of any kind
whatsoever in their Houses; and the Popish
Worship, at the French Factory in their
Neighbourhood, has much confirmed them in
an Opinion that all Christians are Idolaters. But
I shall not say any more here upon this Head,

since their Religion, and the Ceremonies relating to it, are pretty well known.

I might add several other Particulars, concerning their Dress, their Houses, Oeconomy, and the like; but these too being described at large in several Books already published, I shall make an End of this Section, and so pass on.

SECT. IV.

Of JOB's Person and Character.

JOB was about five Feet ten Inches high, strait limb'd, and naturally of a good Constitution; altho' the religious Abstinence which he observed, and the Fatigues he lately underwent, made him appear something lean and weakly. His Countenance was exceeding pleasant, yet grave and composed; his Hair long, black, and curled, being very different from that of the Negroes commonly brought from Africa.

His natural Parts were remarkably good; and I believe most of the Gentlemen that conversed with him frequently, will remember many Instances of his Ingenuity. On all Occasions he discovered a solid judgment, a ready Memory, and a clear Head. And, notwithstanding the Prejudices which it was natural for him to have in favour of his own religious Principles, it was very observable with how much Temper and Impartiality he would reason in Conversation upon any Question of that kind, while at the same Time he would frame such Replies, as were calculated at once to support his own Opinion, and to oblige or please his Opponent. In his Reasonings there appeared nothing trifling, nothing hypocritical or over-strained; but, on the contrary, strong Sense, joined with an innocent Simplicity, a strict Regard to Truth, and a hearty Desire to find it. Tho' it was a considerable Disadvantage to him in Company, that he was not sufficient Master of our Language; yet those who were used to his Way, by making proper Allowances, always found themselves agreeably entertained by him.

The Acuteness of his Genius appear'd upon many Occasions. He very readily conceived the Mechanism and Use of most of the ordinary Instruments which were shewed to him here; and particularly, upon seeing a Plow, a Grist Mill, and a Clock taken to pieces, he was able to put them together again himself, without any farther Direction.

His Memory was extraordinary; for when he was fifteen Years old he could say the whole Alcoran by heart, and while he was here in England he wrote three Copies of it without the Assistance of any other Copy, and without so much as looking to one of those three when he wrote the others. He would often laugh at me when he heard me say I had forgot any Thing, and told me he hardly ever forgot any Thing in his Life, and wondered that any other body should.

In his natural Temper there appeared a happy Mixture of the Grave and the Chearful, a gentle Mildness, guarded by a proper Warmth, and a kind and compassionate Disposition towards all that were in Distress. In Conversation he was commonly very pleasant; and would every now and then divert the Company with some witty Turn, or pretty Story, but never to the Prejudice of Religion, or good Manners. I could perceive, by several slight Occurrences, that, notwithstanding his usual Mildness, he had Courage enough, when there was occasion for it: And I remember a Story which he told me of himself, that is some Proof of it. As he was passing one Day thro' the Country of the Arabs, on his way home, with four Servants, and several Negroes which he had bought, he was attacked by fifteen of the wild Arabs, who are known to be common Bandetti, or Robbers in those Parts. JOB, upon the first Sight of this Gang, prepared for a Defence; and setting one of his Servants to watch the Negroes, he, with the other three, stood on his Guard. In the

Fight one of JOB's Men was killed, and JOB himself was run thro' the Leg with a Spear. However, having killed two of the Arabs, together with their Captain and two Horses, the rest fled, and JOB brought off his Negroes safe.

JOB's Aversion to Pictures of all Sorts, was exceeding great; insomuch, that it was with great Difficulty that he could be brought to sit for his own. We assured him that we never worshipped any Picture, and that we wanted his for no other End but to keep us in mind of him. He at last consented to have it drawn; which was done by Mr. Hoare. When the Face was finished, Mr. Hoare ask'd what Dress would be most proper to draw him in; and, upon JOB's desiring to be drawn in his own Country Dress, told him he could not draw it, unless he had seen it, or had it described to him by one who had: Upon which JOB answered, If you can't draw a Dress you never saw, why do some of you Painters presume to draw God, whom no one ever saw? I might mention several more of his smart Repartees in Company, which shewed him to be a Man of Wit and Humour, as well as good Sense: But that I may not be tedious, what I have said shall suffice for this Head.

As to his Religion, 'tis known he was a
Mahometan, but more moderate in his
Sentiments than most of that Religion are. He
did not believe a sensual Paradise, nor many
other ridiculous and vain Traditions, which
pass current among the Generality of the
Turks. He was very constant in his Devotion to
God; but said, he never pray'd to Mahommed,
nor did he think it lawful to address any but
God himself in Prayer. He was so fixed in the
Belief of one God, that it was not possible, at
least during the Time he was here, to give him
any Notion of the Trinity; so that having had a
New Testament given him in his own
Language, when he had read it, he told me he
had perused it with a great deal of Care, but
could not find one Word in it of three Gods, as
some People talk: I did not care to puzzle him,
and therefore answered in general, that the
English believed only in one God. He shewed
upon all Occasions a singular Veneration for
the Name of God, and never pronounced the
Word Allah without a peculiar Accent, and a
remarkable Pause: And indeed his Notions of
God, Providence, and a future State, were in
the main very just and reasonable.

His Learning, considering the
Disadvantages of the Place he came from, was

far from being contemptible. The Books in his Country are all in Manuscript, all upon Religion; and are not, as I remember, more than Thirty in Number. They are all in Arabick; but the Alcoran, he says, was originally wrote by God himself, not in Arabick, and God sent it by the Angel Gabriel to Ababuker, sometime before Mahommed was born; the Angel taught Ababuker to read it, and no one can read it but those who are instructed after a different Manner from that in which the Arabick is commonly taught. However, I am apt to think that the Difference depends only upon the Pointing of the Arabick, which is of later Date. JOB was well acquainted with the historical Part of our Bible, and spoke very respectfully of the good Men mentioned in Scripture; particularly of JESUS CHRIST, who, he said, was a very great Prophet, and would have done much more Good in the World, if he had not been cut off so soon by the wicked Jews; which made it necessary for God to send Mahomet to confirm and improve his Doctrine.

CONCLUSION;

Containing Some REFLECTIONS upon the whole.

One can't but take Notice of a very remarkable Series of Providence, from the Beginning of JOB's Captivity, till his Return to his own Country. When we reflect upon the Occasion and Manner of his being taken at first, and the Variety of Incidents during his Slavery, which, from slight and unlikely Beginnings, gradually brought about his Redemption, together with the singular Kindness he met with in this Country after he was ransomed, and the valuable Presents which he carried over with him; I say, when all these Things are duly considered, if we believe that the wise Providence of the great Author of Nature governs the World, 'tis natural for us to conclude that this Process, in the divine Oeconomy of Things, is not for nought, but that there is some important End to be served by it.

Our own imperfect Observations have discovered to us innumerable Instances of Design and Contrivance in the natural World;

and tho' we cannot assign the immediate
Causes and Ends of all the Phenomena of
Nature, yet we know enough of them to
convince us that the same uniform Design, the
same wife and beautiful Order is carried on
and maintained throughout the whole. And as
there is a manifest Analogy between the
Methods of Government in the natural and
moral Worlds, so that they seem to be but as
different Acts of the same grand Drama; and
since the Providence of God is no less certain
than his Existence, Chance being as unable to
govern a World as to make one; we may safely,
and on good Grounds infer, that the various
Occurrences in human Life, however
inconsiderable or perplexed they may appear
to us, are neither beneath the Care, nor
inextricable to the Wisdom of him who rules
the Universe: No; they have all their proper
Places in the great Scheme; and all conspire in
a regular Gradation, to bring about their
several Ends, in Subserviency to the whole.

'Tis true, neither the Extent of our Lives
nor Capacities will permit us to view any very
great Part of the Works of God; and what we
do see, we are too apt to put a wrong
Construction upon, being unacquainted in a
great measure with the secret Springs of

Nature, and altogether unable to take in the vast Projects of infinite Wisdom: But the particular Scenes that we are sometime presented with, appear so full of deep Design, and are executed with such divine Art, that they cannot but strike the sober Part of Mankind with Impressions of the highest Wonder, and loudly call for the Attention of a reasonable Being.

History, and our own Experience, furnish us with several amazing Instances of the Conduct of Providence, as well as Nature; which, tho' they cannot be fully or equally accounted for by us, yet may be improved by a well-disposed Mind to very good Purposes; as they serve to increase the high Veneration which we all ought to have for the supreme Lord and Governor of the World, and naturally suggest to us our Dependence upon him; as they tend to confirm our Belief of a Providence, and encourage us to trust our selves entirely in the Hands of our Maker, which is the great Support of every good Man amidst the Calamities of this present Life. In short, as it is very happy for us that the Direction of all Events belongs to God; so we ought to take all Opportunities to excite and strengthen in our selves, and others, a due Sense of his

Government, a becoming Regard to his Works, and just Sentiments of the Relation which we bear to him.

With some such Reflections as these JOB used to comfort himself in his Captivity; and upon proper Occasions, in Conversation, would speak very justly and devoutly of the Care of God over his Creatures, and particularly of the remarkable Changes of his own Circumstances; all which he piously ascribed to an unseen Hand. He frequently compared himself to Joseph; and when he was informed that the King of Futa had killed a great many of the Mandingoes upon his Account, he said, with a good deal of Concern, if he had been there he would have prevented it; for it was not the Mandingoes, but God, who brought him into a strange Land.

It would be Presumption in us to affirm positively what God is about to do at any Time; but may we not be allowed humbly to hope that one End of JOB's Captivity, and happy Deliverance, was the Benefit and Improvement of himself and his People? His Knowledge is now extended to a Degree which he could never have arrived at in his own Country; and the Instruments which he carried over, are well adjusted to the Exigencies of his Countrymen. Who can tell, but that thro' him a whole Nation may be made happy? The Figure which he makes in those Parts, as Presumptive High-priest, and the Interest which he has with the King of the Country, considering the singular Obligations he is under to the English, may possibly, in good time, be of considerable Service to us also; and we have reason to hope this, from the repeated Assurances we had from JOB, that he would, upon all Occasions, use his best Endeavours to promote the English Trade before any other. But whatever be the Consequences, we cannot but please our selves with the Thoughts of having acted so good and generous a Part to a distressed Stranger. And as this gives me occasion to recommend Hospitality, I cannot conclude, without saying something in favour of it.

Among the various Branches of Friendship and Beneficence, there is none of a more noble and disinterested Nature, or that tends more directly to the Union, and consequently the Subsistence of the human Species, than that of Hospitality and Kindness to Strangers. In many Instances of private Friendship, we are apt to be guided by our own private Interest; and very often the

Exchange of good Offices among Friends, is
little better than mere Barter, where an
Equivalent is expected on both Sides. In most
Acts of Charity and Compassion too, we may
be, and very often are wrought upon by the
undue Influence of some selfish View, and
thereby we destroy in good measure the Merit
of them: But in shewing Pity to Strangers, as
such, and kindly relieving them in their
Distress, there is not such Danger of being
influenced by private Regards; nor is it likely
that we are so. Here we act for God's sake, and
for the sake of human Nature; and we seem to
have no Inducement superior to the Will of
Heaven, and the Pleasure that results from the
Consciousness of a generous Respect for our
common Humanity.

There is something singularly sublime,
and even God-like, in this benevolent
Disposition towards Strangers. The common
Parent of the Universe pours out his Blessings
daily upon all Mankind, in all Places of the
Earth; the Just and the Unjust, the Rich and the
Poor, all the Classes, all the Families of human
Creatures, subsist by his Bounty, and have
their Share of his universal Favours. The good
hospitable Man, in his low Sphere, imitates his
Maker, and deals about him to his Fellow

Mortals with great Cheerfulness. He considers his Species in one complex View, and wishes that his Abilities were as extensive as his Inclinations. He does not confine his Benevolence to his Relations, or any particular Party of Men; his Affections are too warm, too general to be thus circumscribed; they must range round the whole Globe, and exert themselves in all Places, where an Opportunity offers.

Such a happy Temper of Mind appeared eminently in those worthy Gentlemen that promoted and encouraged a Subscription for the Relief of JOB; and we hope there are many such Instances of Hospitality among us, which is one very honourable Part of the Character of the English.

FINIS.

16478633R00028

Printed in Great Britain
by Amazon